Carmen's Card

by
Mir Tamim Ansary

Globe
Fearon

Upper Saddle River, New Jersey
www.globefearon.com

Project Editor: Brian Hawkes

Editorial Assistants: Jennifer Keezer, Jenna Thorsland

Art Supervision: Sharon Ferguson

Production Editor: Regina McAloney

Electronic Page Production: José López

Manufacturing Supervisor: Mark Cirillo

Cover Design: Sharon Ferguson

Illustrator: Keaf Holliday

Printed in the United States of America
3 4 5 6 7 8 9 10 04 03 02 01 00

ISBN 0-130-23285-8

Contents

Carmen

Inez

Luis

Tom

1. Getting Out

"I'm off to an apartment sale," says Carmen.

"Don't you have homework?" says her mom.

"I did it, Mom."

"What about your room?" says her sister Inez. "You said you would clean your room."

"Oh, Inez! Get off my back," says Carmen.

"Carmen! Don't talk to your sister that way," says her mom. "Did you clean your room?"

"No—but Mom! I want to get to this sale before all the good things are gone. Can't I clean my room when I get back?"

"OK," says her mom, "but don't forget."

"No way." Carmen moves to the door. But there she runs into her grandma.

"Where are you going, Carmen?" the old woman wants to know. "Don't you want dinner?"

"It's only 3:30!" Carmen points out. "I'll be back long before dinner time."

"OK, but don't forget," says her grandma. "I'm cooking something just for you."

"I'll be here." Carmen has now made it all the way to the hall. But Inez runs after her. "Carmen! Can I come, too?"

"No," says Carmen. "Why do you even ask?"

"Mom! Carmen is being mean to me again!"

"No, Inez," says their mom. "Carmen has a right to go places without you."

Just then, Cougar, the dog, races through the hall. He has something in his mouth.

"Your dog has my homework!" cries Inez.

"**My** dog! Cougar is **your** dog, too!"

"No, he is not. He is your dog! Your name starts with **C**. He is your dog. He has my homework! Do something!"

"Put it down, boy!" Carmen screams at the dog. But Cougar runs away from her fast.

"Get my homework back!" Inez screams.

"I'm trying," says Carmen, as she moves closer to the dog. But Cougar knows what she is up to. He takes off. Carmen lets him go. Cougar has a dog door. He can get outside on his own. That homework is as good as gone. No one will ever see it again. Inez will have to do it over.

Then she hears Inez say, "Oh! Here is my homework after all. The dog didn't get it. That must have been Carmen's homework. Carmen! You have to do your homework over again!"

Carmen thinks, I better get out while I can. She opens the door.

"Carmen!" her mom calls out. But Carmen doesn't hear her. Carmen is outside at last. She is already on her way to the bus stop.

2. The Sale

The sale is in an old apartment. The people are about to move. They are selling things they no longer want. Carmen goes from room to room. She sees an old bike selling for $22. That's just how much money Carmen has. But she doesn't want a bike. It would not be safe around here. There are too many cars. This bike looks old. Forget the bike, thinks Carmen.

In the next room, she sees a CD player. It's pretty new. It works, and it looks good. This is a hot find! But there is one problem. They want $80 for it. Carmen does not have that much money, not even close.

She keeps looking. She finds an old wooden box that is selling for $20. What could she do with a box? She doesn't know. Already, she can hear her sister laughing at her. "Way to go,

Carmen! A wooden box for $20—you really know how to shop!"

But the box is pretty. The longer Carmen looks at it, the more she wants it. $20 for the box: that would leave her $2 for a drink with Tom.

"I'll buy it," she says.

The woman takes her money without a word. Just then a man runs up. "Oh! That's just what I'm looking for. How much for the box, my good woman?"

But the woman says, "I just sold that. Talk to the girl."

He turns to Carmen. "Will you sell me the box? How much do you want for it?"

"Well, I gave her $20 for it."

"Well, look here. I have been looking all over for a box like this. It isn't really worth $20. But I will give you $25 for it. What do you say?"

"How come you will part with $25—for a box that's not worth $20?"

This stops the man. "Well, I just like it," he says at last. "It's—you know, a good-looking box."

"I like it, too." Carmen puts the box into her

bag. She thinks, what's wrong with me? I was thinking $20 was too much. Now I feel like $25 is too little. It's not as if Carmen needs the box. Making money at a sale would be a first. But if the man wants the box, so does Carmen. She can't help it. That's just the way it is.

The man says, "OK, but think about it, will you? If you change your mind, call me. Let me give you my card."

"Keep your card," says Carmen. "I want this box. Sorry."

3. A Big Hit

Carmen leaves the sale. Then she remembers that her boyfriend Tom has a game today. Tom plays baseball. He is on the school team. He is the best player on the team. He is a good-looking guy, too. A lot of girls would like to be in Carmen's place and have Tom for a boyfriend. But going out with Tom is hard in some ways. He wants Carmen to be at all his games. He gets mad when Carmen doesn't make it. Most people would say the game today is not a big one. But Tom says every game is a big game. That's the way he thinks. That—in part—is what makes him so good.

When Carmen gets to the field, the game is just about over. "What's happened?" she asks. A guy tells her about the game. Tom has five hits so far. He has two runs. But his team is behind two to three. Tom is up. There is one player on base.

The game is down to the last out. If Tom doesn't get a hit, it will all be over.

Tom waits for the ball.

"Go, Tom! Get a hit!" Carmen calls out.

Tom looks up. Just then the ball comes. By the time Tom looks back, it's gone.

"Ball one!"

Tom looks a little mad. He puts his mind back into the game. Another ball comes. Now Carmen hears the sound. A hit! It's a good one. The ball goes way, way up. People are screaming, "Run, Tom, run!" But Tom does not really have to race. That ball is gone. He walks around the bases. The game is over. Tom's team has won, four to three. Everyone is trying to get close to Tom. Everyone is laughing. Everyone is talking. "What a game!" "Too much!" "Turn it on, Tom." "Man, you were **hot** today!"

"Way to go, champion." This time it is Carmen.

Tom looks around. "There you are. Did you see the game?"

"Just the end of it. I was at a sale."

Tom's face goes dark. "A sale? Did you forget I had a game today?"

"Sorry, Tom. This was a really good sale."

"This was a really good game! How can you go to some sale on a day when I'm playing? I only play three times a week! You can go to a sale any day."

"No, I can't. This was a one-day sale," she tells him. "But I did see your last hit."

"Well, if you could only see one, that was the one to see." Tom feels a little better. "What did you get at the sale?"

"An old wooden box."

"A box? What for?" Tom doesn't get it.

"I don't know," says Carmen. "It looked good."

"It looked good? Is that all? How much was it?"

"Only $20," says Carmen.

"**Only**! That's a laugh!" he says. "How could some little box be worth $20? Go get your money back, Carmen. Buy something you can use."

"I can use this, Tom. I can put things in it."

"Yes. That's what a box is for. But what things? Why do they have to go in a $20 box? Why can't they go in any old box?"

"It's really pretty," Carmen tells him.

"If you say so," he laughs.

"Laugh all you want," she says. "I could have made money on this box."

"Money?" Tom sits up. "How so?"

"Well, a man wanted the box, too. He asked me to sell it to him for $25."

"You didn't do it? Oh, Carmen! What am I going to do with you? There are times when you can be so—" He tries to find the word. He can't.

"I know what I'm like," says Carmen. "You don't have to say it. If someone else wants a thing, I want it, too. I am what I am."

"That's your problem right there," says Tom. "You are what you are. But it's your money, I guess. Get in the car. Let's go somewhere. I'll buy you a cold drink."

"Where should we go?" she asks.

"How about the same old place?"

"Sounds OK," says Carmen.

4. Money Problems

The same old place is Mom's Home Cooking.
But the name gives the wrong idea. Mom's Home
Cooking has nothing to do with any mom. The
place sells fast food. A big guy by the name of
Dan runs it. Some people call him **Big Dan**.
Others call him **Mom**—just for a laugh. He
doesn't mind. Kids do most of the work. Carmen
herself works there after school. She likes to go
there when she is not working. So do many other
kids from her school. It has nothing to do with
the food. No one likes the food at Mom's. Kids go
there because other kids go there. They know
they will meet up with friends. That's what people
like about Mom's Home Cooking.

Tom gets drinks and comes back to Carmen.
He sits down. It hits Carmen that Tom is sad.
"What's on your mind, Champion?" she asks. "You
would think you just **lost** a game."

Tom gives her a smile. "I was just thinking about money problems."

"What do you mean, money problems?"

"I need money. What else could I mean?"

"You could get a job," she points out. "You could work here at Mom's. Big Dan is looking for someone to clean up."

"I need more than that," Tom says. "But it's a long story. You don't want to hear it."

"Yes, I do," says Carmen.

"Well," Tom starts, "I was talking to Coach before the game today. He was telling me that I'm good."

"Some news!" says Carmen. "Everyone already knows you're the best."

"No, but he means really good. Coach says I could make it to the big time. I could play ball for money. I have what it takes. He called me in just to tell me that. Then he told me about a place up in the mountains. It's like a baseball school, or something. Kids go there for three weeks at a time. They work with a Hall of Fame coach. Every big team has a guy there to see the kids and find new players. So going to this place could be the start of something big. Maybe a big-time team would see me play and ask me to try out. Just like that, I could be on my way to money and fame."

"But that all sounds good, Tom. Why the long face?" Carmen asks.

He gives a laugh. "**Sounds** good—yes. That's just what I said. Coach got me all fired up about this place. What's more, he said I didn't have to do a thing. He knows some people up there. All he has to do is call them, and I would be in. He asked me if he should make that call. I said yes! What else would I say? Then he gave me the bad news."

"Oh, no."

"Oh, yes. It takes money to go to this place— $500. Where am I going to get that? I will not get it working at Mom's. How could I save that much working here? The money for the school has to go in next week. No way can I make $500 that fast."

"Can't you ask your Dad?" Carmen asks. "Your family is pretty well off, Tom."

"My dad?" Tom lets out a hard laugh. "You must be kidding! Dad wants me to give up baseball. He says it's just a game. If Dad had his way, I would be working in his shop after school. That's a real job, as he puts it. No, my dad will not give me money for baseball. I have to do it on my own. That means I can't do it. Coach got me all fired up—and then he let me down. What a guy!"

"I'm sorry," says Carmen. "I would do anything to help. If I had $500, I would give it to you. Because I know I would get it back. I believe in you."

"Good for you," says Tom, "but you don't have the money—do you? So it's just talk. Isn't it? It gets me down. So let's talk about something else for a change."

"Well," says Carmen, "all right." She tries to think of something else to talk about. "What about my box? Do you want to see it now?"

"I guess," says Tom. His face is dark and sad.

5. What Carmen Finds

"Here." Carmen takes the box out of her bag. Tom gives it a look. He turns it over. He looks at the other side. He turns it over again. "Not bad—as boxes go," he says at last. "It's pretty. I'll give you that. But it's just a box. I don't see how it's worth $20."

"Look at the details on it," Carmen says. "It is so well made."

"Well made! So what?" he answers. "It looks used, Carmen. You could get a new one like this for $7.50. I know a place."

"Old is what I like about it, Tom. When I hold this box, I feel like I go back in time."

"Old may be good at times," says Tom. "But this box is so old, it's coming apart."

"Where?" Carmen takes the box back from her boyfriend. He is right. Some of the wood is

"There is something back here," says Carmen.

coming away from the side of the box. Behind this wood, Carmen sees something. She pulls the wood away from the box to get a better look.

"What are you doing?" says Tom. "Be careful!"

"There is something back here," says Carmen.

"Stop playing with the box!" Tom cries out. "By the time you're done, it will be worth nothing."

"It's my box," Carmen says. She pulls at the wood. She gets a hold of the thing she sees. Then she pulls the thing out.

Tom sits up. "What is it? Money? Give it to me. I want to see." He puts out his hand. When he sees what it is, he sits back. "It's just an old baseball card."

"Could it be worth something?" Carmen asks.

"No way," Tom laughs. He reads the name from the card: "Jake Hall. No, Carmen. I don't believe this guy made the Hall of Fame."

"But the card looks old," says Carmen. "You don't know the name of every player that ever did play. Do you?"

Then Tom sees something behind Carmen. "Oh, no," he says, "look what just came through the door."

6. Mad Dog Hall

Luis has just walked into Mom's Home Cooking. Luis looks a little like Tom. But he is not as big. He goes to Carmen's school, but he is not in her class. He wanted to get on the baseball team one time. But he didn't make it. He took Inez out two or three times, but they no longer go together. Inez says she put an end to it. Carmen doesn't know why. Inez has only said, "Oh! Luis is OK. But he is no Tom!" Today, Luis has a little smile on his face. He looks around the room, taking his time.

"Why are you so down on Luis?" Carmen asks her boyfriend.

"What's to like?" Tom answers. "Luis the Mouth. He is all talk. Forget him."

By this time, Luis has seen Carmen and Tom.

He is walking over to them. "What's the word, Champion?" he says to Tom.

Tom does not answer. He hardly even looks at Luis. Carmen has to do all the talking. "Nothing much. What are you up to, Luis?"

"Same old, same old," says Luis. "Say, do you know about any cars for sale? I have been looking for one all day. Man, that can wear you down!"

"You're going to buy a car?" says Carmen.

"I want to. You can't get much for $500, it turns out."

Tom looks up. "You have $500? Where did you get that much money?"

"I worked for it, man. I paint, you know. I do an ad on this shop window every week."

"Oh." Tom looks down again. This is not a way that **he** can make fast money.

"What have you got in your hand?" Luis asks Carmen.

"It's an old baseball card." Carmen holds it up.

Luis reads from the card: "Jake Hall." He says, "Wait! Could this be **Mad Dog Hall?**"

"Who is Mad Dog Hall?" Carmen wants to know.

"He is a player from a long time back. I don't know why they called him Mad Dog. If this is the same Jake Hall, the card could be worth something, Carmen."

Tom looks at him. "Get out of here, Luis! Mad Dog Hall! You're making up another one."

"No, really," says Luis. "Mad Dog Hall. He started way back in 1897."

"How do you know that?"

"It says so." Luis points to the back of the card. "Right there."

The others look. There it is, all right: 1897.

"A card this old has got to be worth something," Luis says.

"He is right, you know." Carmen turns to Tom.

Tom just laughs again. "Why don't you buy the card, if it's worth so much."

"How about it?" Luis asks Carmen. "I'll give you $20 for that card. Right here, right now."

7. That Man Again!

Just then, a dog comes up to Carmen. "Cougar!" she cries. "What are you doing here?" If Cougar is here, can Inez be far behind? Carmen looks around, and yes, there is her sister Inez. Carmen knows why she has come to Mom's Home Cooking. She wants to see Tom. She knows she will find him here with Carmen. Tom is Carmen's boyfriend. But does that stop Inez? Not at all. She likes him all the more for it. Inez wants everything that Carmen has.

Tom waves to Inez. Inez waves back. She says, "I hear you won the game today. All by yourself, from what I hear."

"Yes, I did, kid. I had a big hit in the 9th—right out of the field, over the houses—home run. You should have been there. How did you hear about it?"

"Oh, everyone knows already. They are all talking about you," says Inez. "That's my Tom!"

"He is not really your Tom," Carmen points out.

Carmen is 16. Inez is 14. Many boys like Inez, but Inez can take or leave most of them. It's Tom she likes. Would she like him if he were not Carmen's boyfriend? No one knows the answer to that one. Carmen gets mad at times. But what can she do? Way down inside, she knows how Inez feels. Carmen is the same way herself. She did not want the box at first. Someone else had to want it before she did. The baseball card was nothing to her. Luis had to want it first. Yes, Carmen knows how her sister feels. She and her sister are alike in a lot of ways.

Then she sees Tom. Inez is going on and on to him. He must like what he hears. His face is all light and happy. "Inez," he says, "I must say, you're looking good today. I like what you're wearing."

"Oh, this old thing?" says Inez, looking down at herself.

"Inez, that old thing you're wearing happens to be my old thing. I did not say you could put it on." Carmen tries to sound cold. "What do you want here, anyway?"

Inez hears the words. But she doesn't feel the cold. "Mom told me to come and get you. You said you were going to clean your room, and you didn't."

"Oh, no!" Carmen remembers what she said.

"Grandma made dinner," Inez goes on. "You said you would be home. But you didn't make it. Grandma is all sad now."

"Oh, no! How could I forget again?"

Inez goes on. "Do you know when Cougar got my homework?"

"I know. I know. It was my homework. I have to do it over." Carmen looks at Tom. "Believe it or not, this started as a good day." To Inez, she says, "Go on home, Inez. Tell them I'm coming. Oh, and take Cougar with you. He should not be here in Mom's."

"Don't tell me what to do with Cougar," says Inez. "He is my dog."

"Oh? At home, you said he was my dog."

"I know. At home, he is your dog. Out here, he is my dog."

Just then a boy cries out. "Who owns that dog? It just got away with my food. You there—girl. Yes—you!" He is looking at Inez. "Is this your dog?"

Inez gets scared. "No—not really. It's more her dog." She points to Carmen.

Carmen thinks, What do you do with a sister like Inez?

The boy goes on. "Don't you give me that story, little girl. I saw the dog come in with you. Are you going to give me some money for my food?"

Carmen gets mad at that boy. She is up fast. She is in his face. "Maybe you don't hear her? She told you it's my dog. Don't you ever talk to my sister like that!"

"Or what?" The boy comes closer.

"Or you will have to answer to me," says Tom. Tom doesn't get up. He doesn't have to. Everyone around here knows Tom. Fame helps at times. The boy backs down. "Oh—Tom. Man. I didn't see you. These girls with you? I didn't know, Champion. It's just that—I came in here for a little food, you know? My last $2! Now my food is gone and my money, too. You know?"

Luis calls out from the back of the room. "What did you have? I'll buy you another." He walks over, taking out his money.

But Carmen says, "No, Luis. What are you doing? This is not your problem." To Inez, she says, "Get that dog out of here, will you? Do it fast."

"I'll wait outside." Inez walks out with Cougar. Carmen makes Luis put his money away. "Look," she tells the boy, "I'm sorry about my dog. I'll make it up to you. But there was no need to talk about hitting people."

"I didn't mean anything by it." The boy takes her last $2. He goes away happy. Carmen says, "Well, I better get going. I'll—"

She stops.

"What?" says Tom.

"Look over there," she says.

"I'm looking," he says. "I see a man. So what?"

"Remember what I told you about the sale? There was a man who wanted to give me $25 for the box."

"What about him?"

"That's him," says Carmen. "That man over there. That's him."

"OK. So it's him. Why do you look scared?" says Tom. "There is nothing to be scared of. He is just some guy."

"Yes, but think about it," she says. "He was there. I was there. I come here—and so does he. I just don't like it."

"Lighten up!" Tom laughs. "Do you think he is after you! He just came in here for some food, like everyone else."

"Who comes to Mom's for the food?" Carmen says. "He is too old to be in here."

"You don't have to be a kid to be in here," Tom answers her.

"No, but look around. What do you see? Kids and more kids. Oh, Tom. He is coming this way!" Carmen gets up.

Tom gets up, too. "I'll drive you home. Will that make you feel better?" The man stops when he sees that they are going. But he is looking at them as they leave.

Outside, Inez is happy to see Tom with Carmen. "Oh, good! Is Tom taking us home?"

"Not all of us," says Tom. "My car is too little for three people and a dog. Anyway, I don't want a dog in my car."

"I know what," says Inez, "Carmen can take Cougar home. I will go with you, Tom."

"Think again," says Carmen. She moves around her sister and gets into the car. As Tom pulls away, Carmen looks back. "Well, I don't see that guy."

"See," says Tom. "What did I tell you? He was not after you."

8. Good News for Carmen

Carmen's grandma is at the door when Carmen gets home. "Dinner is cold," she says. "Where were you?"

"I'm sorry, Grandma." Carmen feels bad. "I was at Mom's Home Cooking with Tom."

"Mom's Home Cooking—that's a laugh," says grandma. "The idea of that man calling himself Mom. And he calls that place home? It's not even a house! And cooking? Don't even talk to me about it. They just take food out of a can and get it hot. We didn't call that cooking in my day."

"We don't call it cooking now, Grandma." Carmen likes her grandma. She wants to make her happy. "We just go there to be with other kids. I like your cooking the best. Your food is hot, even when it's cold."

"Oh!" says her grandma. "The things you say!" But Carmen has made her feel better.

"Where is your sister?" Grandma asks.

"She is walking home with Cougar."

"That dog is nothing but a problem," says Grandma.

"Oh, Grandma. Cougar is a good dog."

"You call him good? That dog is always taking things. One day, he got a hold of your mom's sleeping bag. What he did to that bag was sad. Oh, it was just sad. He took my ring, too."

"Grandma, we only know that your ring is lost," Carmen starts in. "We don't really know that Cougar—"

"Oh, he took it all right. I guess it looked like dog food to Cougar. My first boyfriend gave me that ring, and it ends up inside a dog! Oh, I tell you. I would throw that dog right out of this house, if only it were up to me."

"So you say, Grandma. But when did you ever forget to give Cougar his food?" Carmen smiles.

"Oh, well. A dog needs food, same as people." Grandma puts her hands together.

"You let Cougar sleep in your room," says Carmen.

"What of it?" says Grandma. "Every dog needs a place to sleep."

"In your room?" says Carmen.

"He has to sleep somewhere," says Grandma.

"I think you like Cougar," says Carmen.

"Oh! The idea! Me? That dog? Not!" The old woman gets up and walks away, talking to herself.

After dinner, Carmen shows the family her box. No one thinks much of it. Her mom says, "Well, it's your money."

Her grandma says, "$20! For a box? In my day, a box like that was only $1."

Inez just laughs. She says, "You lost $20 on this box. Look. It's coming apart already."

Carmen does not tell her family about the card. She is going to wait. She wants to know more about it first. But in her room that night, she can't stop thinking about what Luis has said. Luis likes to talk, she knows. He will say anything, if it makes a good story. But what if he is right this time? She is thinking about this, as she goes to sleep.

34

The next day Carmen takes the card to a shop that sells baseball cards. A little old man runs it. He takes a close look at Carmen's card. "Not bad," he says. "Are you looking to sell this? I could part with $30 for it."

Carmen's feelings start to race. $30! If she sells it now, she will have $10 more than she started with. She thinks about the people who have been laughing at her. But something keeps her from saying yes. So she says, "$30? Don't make me laugh! Look again! That's a Mad Dog Hall card."

"Oh." The man looks up. "You know about Mad Dog Hall, do you?"

"Like the back of my hand," says Carmen.

"You know about baseball cards, too?"

"I know a thing or two," says Carmen. "Now tell me what the card is really worth."

"I'm sorry," says the man. "I did try to put one over on you. Money does things to a guy. But I'll come clean with you now. The card is worth a lot. I guess you know that."

"Yes. But how much is a lot?"

"How does $20,000 sound?"

9. Being Careful

Carmen's mind stops working. Did she hear him right? She must not show how she feels. She has to play this just right. She tries to look as if she is thinking it over. In the end, she says, "Well, $20,000 sounds OK, but $25,000 sounds even better."

"OK. Maybe $25,000," says the man. "But don't forget. Selling a thing like this is a lot of work. It's not like selling a used car. You can't just run an ad. You can't let someone come to your house and look at it. By and by, the wrong people would come over. Where did you get this thing, anyway?"

"It's my card. That's all you need to know."

"OK. OK. Don't get mad. I just asked. Anyway, you want my thinking? Sell the card to me. I will be happy to buy it for $22,000."

"What will you do with it?" Carmen asks.

"I will keep it while I wait for the right guy to come along. Then I'll sell it."

"For how much?"

"As much as I can get," the man says. "$25,000 or more."

"Well, then," says Carmen. "Why should I sell it to you? Why don't **I** keep the card? I can wait for the right guy to come along."

The man laughs. "He will not come to you. Selling baseball cards is a game, girl. I know people who have money and buy cards. I can call them up. You can't. Take my word for it. You need my help to sell this box. You want to make money, don't you?"

Carmen thinks for a while. "OK," she says. "I see your point. But I can't sell the card today. I want to shop around a little first."

"I can't buy it today, anyway," the man says. "It will take me two or three days to get that much money together. So talk to other shops if you want. Find out what they will give you. But don't sell the card. OK? I'll call you in a day or two. Tell me what you can get from the others. I will see if I can do better. If I can't, too bad for me."

"OK," says Carmen. "I'll hold on to the card for now. Let's talk again in a day or two."

"But girl," he says, "one more thing."

"Yes?" Carmen turns.

"Be careful," he says. "Don't go telling lots of people about the card. I'm a good guy. Some people are not so good. You know?"

"I know. I know." But Carmen thinks no one has to tell me a thing like that. Who does this guy think he is?

She races home. She feels like laughing and screaming at the same time. She runs into her house. "$22,000!" she cries out.

"What?" No one in her family knows what she is talking about. She waves the card around. It's a long time before she can really tell them what has happened.

Her mom laughs. "Oh, come on, Carmen. Who is going to believe a story like that?"

Grandma says, "$22,000 for one card? In my day, you could get 52 cards for $1.00."

"This isn't from a pack of playing cards, Grandma. This is a baseball card. It's old. There is no other one like it," Carmen says.

"I'm old," says her grandma, "and there is no other one like me. Am I worth $22,000?"

"You're worth $22,000,000," says Carmen. "But you have a point. I don't know why an old card should be worth so much. It just is."

Carmen's mom stops laughing. "You mean this is not a story?"

Now at last her family starts to believe her. They are happy for her. Even Inez says, "Oh, Carmen! You really know how to shop!"

Right away they have ideas about what she should do with the money. Grandma says, "Now we can do the kitchen over. Get your mom a new sleeping bag, too. Then my ring—"

"No," says her mom, "Carmen is going to put the money away. She can use it for college, or maybe she can start a little shop when she gets out of school."

Inez is just looking at Carmen. But Carmen knows she will come up with ideas before long. Carmen doesn't want to hear them just now. "I'm going to call Tom," she says.

10. Tom Gets Mad

Tom answers after one ring.

"Guess what!" Carmen screams.

"What?" says Tom.

"You know that baseball card? I took it to a card shop. Guess what it's worth."

"A lot, I would guess," Tom smiles. "From the way you sound."

"A lot could be anything. Guess how much," she says.

"$100?"

"Try again," she says.

"$200?"

Carmen laughs. "Think big, Tom. Think $22,000!"

When Tom hears these words, he feels all hot inside. Then he feels all cold. Then hot again. $22,000! Could it really be? Well, then. This is the end of his money problems. He can go to that baseball place after all. Carmen can give him the money!

"Tom?" says Carmen. "Are you there? Did you hear me?"

"Yes," says Tom. "I don't know what to say. I can hardly take it in." Then he gets scared. Maybe Carmen got it wrong. It would not be the first time. "Carmen—" he says, "can you believe this guy at the card shop. Does he really know what he is talking about? Maybe you didn't hear him right. Maybe he said $22, not $22,000."

"Oh, he said $22,000 all right," Carmen tells her boyfriend. "He wants to buy it himself. He is trying to get the money together right now. Selling baseball cards is what he does for work. He must know what he is talking about. I tell you, Tom, this is money in the bank."

So now, at last, Tom starts to believe. He says, "Don't move, Carmen. I am coming over. At a time like this, we should be together."

Tom gets into his car. But on the way to Carmen's house, he gets to thinking, what if Carmen does not want to give him the money? She said she would do anything to help him. But that was then. This is now. What if she does not feel the same way now?

I can't just ask her, Tom thinks. What if she says no? Anyway, it would not be good to ask for money right away. Everyone will be doing that. Tom will be just one more guy with his hand out. That picture makes Tom feel little. He isn't used to that feeling. He doesn't like it.

No, he thinks, I had better let her tell me how much she will give me and when. She knows my problem. She knows how much this baseball school means to me. She must be thinking about it already. Yes, that must be it. She can hardly wait to tell me that she will give me some money. She would not make me come to her and ask for money. I'm her boyfriend, after all. She would not do that to me.

When Tom gets to Carmen's house, she races up to him. She looks as happy as can be. She starts talking right away. But she does not say anything about the money he needs.

"Well," says Tom at last, "let me see this hot card." Carmen gives it to him. "Boy," he says, looking at it, "who was this Jake Hall, anyway?"

"I read up on him today," says Carmen. "Jake was only in 20 games. All in 1897. He hit seven home runs in one game. People said he could be the best ever. But a bad thing happened. One day, a mad dog got out on the field somehow. Jake and one other guy could not get away from it. One week after that, he got sick. A week after that he was gone. That's why they called him Mad Dog Hall. Well, a story like that is big news for a while. But then people forget. Everyone knows some Jake Hall cards were made. But over time, they all got lost. This is the first one to ever turn up. That's why it's worth so much money."

"What a story," says Tom. He waits for Carmen to go on and talk about the $500 he needs.

But Tom's baseball school is the last thing on Carmen's mind right now. Tom tries to get her to talk about it. He says, "What are you going to do with all that money?"

"I don't know," she laughs. "I don't even want to think about it right now. What if the card does not sell or something? I want the money in my hand."

"Oh," says Tom. Then he thinks, she could have said it right then. But she didn't. She must not want to give me anything, and after all that I have done for this girl! What's wrong with her?

Carmen asks Tom if he wants some food. He says he doesn't. She asks him if he wants something to drink. He says no. She tells him how her grandma wants a new sleeping bag. "Boy, they are all going to line up," she laughs. "I have to be careful."

Tom starts to look sad. Carmen goes on to talk about her dog. Tom looks even more sad. He is waiting to hear about his $500. Carmen does not know that. She just sees his long face.

"What's wrong?" she asks at last.

"Nothing," says Tom. He does not want to let his feelings show. Carmen is not going to help me, he thinks. It's hard to believe! It makes me feel so bad.

"Well!" says Carmen. "Can't you work up a smile or something? This is a big day for me, you know!"

"For you! For you! Yes! A big day for **you**!" Tom cries out. "What about other people? Why don't you try thinking about someone else for a change?"

"Someone else? Tom! What's got into you? Who do you mean?"

Tom just looks at her. His mouth is open. He can't believe it. This baseball school is the biggest thing that ever happened to him, and Carmen does not even remember about it! This just goes to show how little he means to her. She comes into some money. Right away, her boyfriend is nothing to her. He is so mad now that he can hardly talk. At last, he gets some words out. "What about—" But he stops. He can't talk about himself now. It will not sound good. It will sound like he is just after money. "What about Inez?" he says at last.

Inez? Carmen thinks. What is this about Inez? She starts to get mad. Do Tom and Inez have something going on behind her back? "Look," she says. "It's my money. OK? Didn't you all laugh at me and say the box was a bad buy? Didn't you all say the card was worth nothing? Well, you all were wrong. Now you try to tell me what to do with the money? What gives you the right?"

Tom's mouth opens. Not a word comes out. His look is hot and dark. Then at last, he says, "That's it. I'm out of here. I'm not going to sit here and take this. Have a good time with your money, Carmen. I mean it. Have a good, good time." Tom gets up and leaves.

Carmen runs to the window and throws it open. "Tom," she cries. But he keeps going. "Boy!" she says. "What is wrong with that guy?"

Inez smiles. "I guess he thinks you're being mean to me. He is right, you know."

11. In the Dark of Night

Carmen doesn't believe Inez. This can't be about her. But what is Tom's problem, then? Is he mad about the card? Why should he be? After all, that card is going to get him into his baseball school. What more does he want? Carmen just doesn't get it. She goes to get her card.

"Where are you going with that?" her mom wants to know.

"To my room," says Carmen.

"Now, Carmen. That card is worth a lot of money," says her mom. "You can't just leave it around, like you do with your things. You have to be more careful. You hear me? You take that card to a bank where it will be safe."

"OK. But I can't do it now," Carmen points out. "Doesn't the bank close by 4:00 today? It's not open on Saturday. I will have to hide the card for now."

"Where?" says her mom.

"How about in this box of old letters?" says Carmen.

"That should work," says her mom.

"But don't tell where it is," says Carmen. "OK, mom? Not even Inez or Grandma."

"Now you're thinking," says her mom. "Hide it in the letter box for now. But get it to a bank as fast as you can. We will go together, you and me."

That night, Carmen can't sleep. There are too many sounds. She hears boys laughing, far away. She hears a big truck go by. She keeps thinking about the card and Tom and things she could buy. Her mind will not stop.

At one point, she hears a car. The sound goes up and down. It sounds like this: RRRRrrrr RRRRrrrrRRRRrrrrRRRRrrrr

She knows that sound from some place. But she can't remember where. When she tries to think about it, her mind moves to other things— to Tom and Luis and the card.

At last, she goes to sleep.

But then she is up again. How long was she sleeping? She doesn't know. She is up now, and she is scared. That's all she knows. The room is dark. She feels cold. She remembers the card. Well, she thinks, the card is safe. No one knows where it is. Then she hears a sound. Someone is talking. She goes to the window to look out. But no one is out there.

Then she hears the sound again. It is not outside. It is coming from somewhere in the house. Who could be in the house? There must be two people. One guy would not be talking. But wait. Now she hears someone walking. Whoever it is comes close to her door. He is right outside. Carmen feels sick. She sees a big wooden ball. I could throw that when he comes in, she thinks. She takes the ball in her two hands.

But the man does not come in. She can hear him going away.

Carmen thinks about calling for help. But she thinks, who would hear me? She opens her door and looks out. There is no one in the dark hall. She moves into the hall and down to the right. Then she sees a light. It's in the kitchen below. Well, the card is not in the kitchen, she thinks. She goes down to see who it is.

She stops at the kitchen door. Her sister is

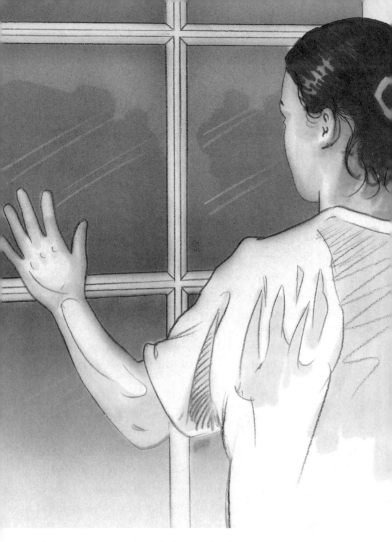

Carmen goes to the window to look out. But no one is there.

drinking something hot. She is looking at the little TV in the kitchen. Some talk show is on. "Inez!" says Carmen. "What are you doing up at this time? You scared me!"

"I'm sorry. I could not sleep. I just came down to get a drink."

"Been up long?" asks Carmen.

"Not too long," says Inez.

"Was that you just now?" Carmen looks at Inez. "Was that you in the hall?"

"Just now?" says Inez. "Yes. I guess."

"Did you come real close to my door?"

"Yes. I wanted to find out if you were sleeping," says Inez.

"Why?" Carmen asks.

Inez does not answer for a while. Then she says, "I was scared, OK? Laugh if you want. I'll say it again. I was scared."

"I'm not laughing," says Carmen. "Why were you scared?"

"I don't know. I guess that card in the house makes me feel a little scared," says Inez. "All that money! Anyway, something got me up. There was

51

a sound or something while I was sleeping. I was thinking you and I could talk. It would make me feel better. I'm happy that you're down here with me now, Carmen. Tell me—what are you going to do with the money? If you ever sell the card, I mean."

"I don't know, Inez. Why? Is there something you want?"

"Oh, Carmen! Would you?" Inez's face lights up. "I saw something really pretty in a shop the other day. It was only $60. Would you buy it for me? I mean, you're going to have so much money! $72 will be like nothing to you."

"$72?" says Carmen. "Didn't you say $60?"

"Well," say Inez. "There is this $12 thing that goes with the $60 thing. I mean, you can't buy one without the other. See? So the two things together—that's $72. But Carmen! You will have so much money! I mean, $72 will be like nothing to you. Right?"

"Right. I will get them for you," says Carmen. But she is thinking, let's see. That's $500 for Tom's baseball school. That's $72 for Inez. Maybe $1,000 for the kitchen, $150 for Mom's sleeping bag. Who else will ask for something? So far I only know what I am going to buy for other people. What am I going to buy for me?

12. The Open Window

Carmen gets up. The sun is out. The day feels clean, but cold. Carmen runs down to take a look at her card. But right away, she sees something bad. The box of letters is open. The letters are all over the place.

Someone did come into the house in the night.

Carmen races to the box. She puts the letters back one by one. But she does not find the card. "Mom!" she screams.

Her mom runs in. Her sister and grandma are close behind. "What is it, Carmen?"

"Mom—!" Carmen feels like crying. "It's gone! The card—Someone took it!"

Her mom sees the open box of letters. "What do you mean, gone? It's in there. You must be wrong. Just wait. I'll find it." She starts to look through the letters.

"It's no use," says Carmen. "I looked at all of them. It's just not there. The box was open. Someone came into our house last night."

"But how could they?" says Inez.

Carmen looks up. Then it hits her. "Inez," she says. "Inez, Inez! Why would you do this thing to me? Where is it?"

"What do you mean?" Inez moves away from Carmen. "You think I took your card?"

"You were down here in the night."

"Well, so were you!" says Inez.

"But you were down here first," says Carmen. "You came by my door to see if I was sleeping. You said so yourself. Why did you want to know if I was sleeping?"

"I told you why! I was scared. I wanted to talk to you. You're my sister! Why would I take your card?"

"Why? Because it's worth $22,000. But you would take it even if it was worth $2. You want every little thing I have. Maybe you just like to see me scared. Maybe you just want to get back at me."

"Get back at you for what?" Inez says.

"You tell me. What did I ever do to you, Inez?"

"You want to know? All right, I'll tell you. Where should I start? You don't let me come with you when you shop. You make me walk the dog. What about that time—"

"Girls!" Carmen's mom sounds mad. "This is not the time or place! Inez, you know how your sister must be feeling! Get off her back. Carmen—how could you say your sister took your card? It's got to be around the house somewhere. Just look for it."

"But this is where I put it," Carmen answers back. "Where else would it be? Why was my letter box open? I tell you someone was in the house last night!"

Just then, they hear a ring. "I'll get it," says Carmen. It's the man from the card shop calling. "Carmen?" he says. "I wanted to get back to you. I can get the money we talked about. But it will take me another day or two. Can you hold out that long?"

"I can't sell the card at all now," says Carmen. "It's lost."

"Oh?" says the man. "Didn't I tell you to be careful?"

"I was careful!" says Carmen. "What more could I do? Someone got into my house and took it."

"Well," says the man. "That's too bad."

Carmen goes back to her family. She tells them about the call. "He did not sound all that sorry," she says. Then it hits her. "That's it!" she cries out. "That man from the shop took my card!"

"What?" says her mom.

"What?" says Inez.

"Don't you see? He knows what the card is worth. He knows I had it. He did try to buy it for next to nothing, you know. When that didn't work, he told me not to sell it. He told me to keep it at home. He told me not to tell about it, and that same night someone gets into the house and takes my card? Oh, I see it all now! Get out of my way, Inez. I have to call the cops."

Carmen's mom gets in her way. "You're not calling the cops. Carmen, this card has done something to your mind. First, you say your sister took it. Now you say this man took it. Does he even know where your house is?"

"Well—" Carmen can't answer that one. "But—But who else knows about the card? Just us and Tom."

"There are some kids at school," says Inez.

"What?" says Carmen.

"Well, it was big news," says Inez. "I just had to tell someone. So I called Luis—"

"Luis!"

"Yes, and some other kids."

"There you go," says Carmen's mom. "Lots of people know about the card. Anyway, no one got into the house. How could they? The door is not—"

"Forget the door," says Carmen. "Look at this." She points to the window. "It's open."

"Well, I'll be!" says Grandma. "Did I Leave it open?"

"Was it me?" says Inez.

But then Carmen remembers. "No," she says, "it was me."

13. The Car

Then Carmen remembers something else. She remembers the car outside the house last night. She remembers the sound of it, too: RRRRrrrrRRRRrrrrRRRRrrrrRRRRrrrr

In the night, she could not place that sound. But now she remembers. It was a car she has been in many times. It was Tom's car.

Carmen feels just sick. Could it be that Tom got into the house? Tom would know his way around.

Then she stops herself. Her mom was right. The card has done something to her mind. How could she even be thinking a thing like this about Tom? She has not even talked to him. She calls his house. He is not home. She calls his friends. He is not with them.

Maybe he is at Mom's Home Cooking, she thinks. So she takes a bus to Mom's. She sees Tom. He sees her as she comes through the door. He looks away—as if he doesn't even know her. She can't see his face. She can't tell what he is thinking. She starts into the room. But Tom gets up and moves away fast. Is he trying to get away from her? Tom leaves through a side door.

"Tom!" Carmen can't let him go like this. She races after him. "Tom!" She screams the words. He turns and looks at her. But then he just keeps going.

"Don't you run away from me," she screams. She races to get a hold of his hand. She makes him stop. "Look at me! Will you? I have to ask you something. Did you come by my house last night?"

"No," he says.

"Tom! Don't do this. I know the sound of your car!"

He stops. "What about my car?"

"Your car was outside my house last night. I would know that sound any place."

"You want to know about my car?" he says. "I'll

tell you about my car." He is really worked up. "I sold my car. Want to know what I got for it? Only $500. Do you know why? Because I needed money fast, and there was no other way to get it. No other way—get me? My so-called **friends** would not help me."

"But, Tom," says Carmen, "how could you do that right after I told you about the card? In a day or two we were going to have lots of money!"

"We? You said it was your money. You told me not to think I was getting any of it."

"What? I didn't say anything like that!"

"Not in so many words. But I got the point."

"Tom! I was going to give you the money!"

"Then why didn't you say so?" he cries out. "Why did you let me sell my car for next to nothing?"

Carmen just looks at him. "I did tell you. How many times do I have to say it?"

"When?" says Tom.

"After the game," says Carmen. "Remember? You told me you needed $500. I said I would do anything to help."

"Oh, but that was before you had any money," Tom says. "How can you give away money that you don't have? Things change when money comes into the picture. We all know that."

"Nothing was going to change." Carmen sounds sad. "I was going to give you the money. To me, that goes without saying. You had my word on it. But what's the use of talking about it now? The card is gone."

"What!" Tom looks like he is about to pass out.

"Yes," says Carmen. "You lost your car. I lost my card. I guess we are even."

"You lost it? Carmen! What's wrong with you? How could you do this to me?"

"Tom, I already feel bad. Where do you get off screaming at me?"

"OK, OK. But try to see how I feel," says Tom. "I mean this is the end. My car is gone because of you. If you were getting money, you could make it up to me. Then I could buy my car back. Because that's what I worked out with Luis. He said he would let me buy the car back—for $650. But only if I could get the money in a week. Can you believe that guy? My back was to the wall. So he used that. But now! Look where I am now!

Now Luis gets to keep my car. For $500! Because of you!"

"Luis?" Carmen says. "You sold your car to Luis?"

"I didn't want to, but he had the money. What else could I do?"

"Did he know about the card?" Carmen feels like she has to sit down. It must have been Luis, then. Luis was outside her house last night. Not Tom. Not the man from the card shop.

Luis.

14. Luis Tells His Story

Carmen takes a bus to Luis's apartment house. It is the first time Carmen has been there. But Inez has told her about it. So Carmen knows what she will find. The place is big and dark. There is wood over one window. There is graffiti all over the outside walls. Carmen sees the words, "Make way for Graffiti Guy!" It looks like something Luis would write.

Carmen goes into the hall. There, she sees more graffiti. She finds Luis's door. Before she can ring, a big man opens the door.

"What do you want?" he says.

Carmen feels a little scared. "Is this—Could I talk to Luis?"

The man turns. "Luis!" he calls. "Get out here, boy. Some girl is looking for you."

Luis comes out. When he sees Carmen, a smile lights up his face. "Well, well, well," he says. "Night turns into day. What's a pretty girl like you doing in a place like this?"

Carmen takes a look at the big man.

"Don't mind Dad," says Luis.

"Luis. Could we talk?" Carmen asks.

"I would like nothing better. Let's go for a drive. I have a car now."

"I know. That's what I want to talk about."

"Did Tom ask you to come? Does he want his car back already? Tell him it will be $650. Just like we said."

"This is not about Tom," says Carmen.

"Oh? Well get into the car then. Let's talk as we drive." Luis smiles at Carmen, as he gets the car started. "What's the story, then?"

"Luis—" But she can't say it. She just can't. If Luis took the card, Carmen will feel sad. She likes Luis. She did not know this before, but she knows it now. He has done some bad things, yes. But nothing really bad. He talks about himself too much, yes. But that's like a game he plays. He shows off a lot, yes. But every time he comes around, Carmen feels better. Nothing gets him down. He makes her laugh. But if he took the card, she can't be friends with him. Not ever.

"Go on—say it. You like me better than any other guy. Right?" says Luis. "Don't hold back. I feel the same way. About me, I mean. I don't know of one guy I like better than me. If only there were two of me, I always say. Then I could be my own best friend! Oh—but did I tell you? There **is** someone I like better. Only she is not a guy. She has a sister by the name of Inez. She—"

"Stop this, Luis. I didn't come to hear you talk to me like this."

"Don't get mad, Carmen. I'm just talking, while you make up your mind to say something."

Then at last the words come out of Carmen. They come fast. "Luis, did you drive by my house last night?"

He says nothing for a while. He just drives. Then he gives his answer. "Yes. I was there."

"Why?"

"Because of that baseball card."

66

"Oh, Luis." She feels like crying now. This is just what she did not want to hear. "Oh, Luis." What can she say next?

But it is Luis who says the next words. "I just wanted to see that you were safe. A card like that is big money. Big money is going to pull in a bad guy, or more than one. Even if you don't tell, somehow the wrong people hear about it. When Inez called **me**, I could tell she must be calling **everyone**. But it was more than that. Remember the man you saw at Mom's? The one from the sale? The guy who wanted to buy the box from you?"

"How could I forget?" Carmen says.

"Well," Luis goes on, "maybe I should have told you this before. But remember that day at Mom's? When you walked out, that guy got up, too. To me, there was something not right about him. So I walked along behind him. Just to see where he would go, you know? When he got into a car, I got on my bike. There were so many cars he could not go all that fast. So I had no problem keeping up with him. You were with Tom. The man was behind you. I was going along behind him."

"But I looked back," says Carmen. "I did not see him."

"He did not mean for you to see him," says Luis. "He was three or four cars back. But in the end, he did pull up by your house. You were inside, I guess. He got out and looked at your house. I saw hin write something down. Then he got back into his car. When Inez told me about the card, I got scared for you. Some people will do anything for money. I got to thinking about this man. I put it all together."

Carmen listens, as Luis tells his story.

"Then I said, he tries to buy the box from Carmen at the sale. She will not sell it. Carmen goes to Mom's. He shows up. She goes home. He goes after her. The guy wants something. He must know about the card. What if he attacks Carmen? I could not sleep thinking about this. In the end, I just had to come by and see that you were OK. I know I'm not your boyfriend. It's not my place to look out for you. Maybe you don't even think of me as a friend. But I didn't really do it for you, Carmen. I did it for me. It makes me feel better to know that you're OK. Is that so wrong?"

"Well, no." Carmen does not know what she thinks about all this. "But can I really believe you, Luis?"

He laughs. "Why not? Why would I make up a thing like that?"

"You didn't get into my house last night? You didn't take my card?"

"What?" The words hit Luis like a baseball. "Someone took your card? What happened? How! Tell me!"

Carmen tells Luis the story from start to end. Then she says, "Look, Luis. I'm sorry. It's not that I think you're a bad guy. It's just that my card is gone, and I feel just sick about it. You were outside my house—"

"Forget about it," says Luis. "What else could you think? You had to ask." Then he says, "There he is again."

"Who?" says Carmen.

"The man from the sale. The one you saw at Mom's. The one I saw at your house. Don't look now. He is behind us."

Carmen does look back. Luis is right. It's that same man. "But Luis," she says, "if he got my card, why is he after me now? What more could he want?"

"I don't know. Let's find out." Luis makes his car go really fast. Then he turns hard. The man behind them can't make the same turn. His car goes on by. Luis laughs. "So far, so good," he says. "Now, let's go after him."

"Can we?" says Carmen. "Should we?"

"We can," says Luis. "We should. He thinks he saw us run away. The last place he will look for us is right behind him. Let's see where he goes. Maybe we can find out who he is."

"I'm game, if you are," says Carmen.

15. Time for the Cops

Luis turns the car around. They find the man. They drive along behind him. He keeps going and going. At last, he pulls over. Luis does, too. The man gets out and starts to walk.

Carmen and Luis get out and go after him.

The man goes into a shop. Luis reads the name of the shop: Time After Time. "What is this?" he says.

"It's a shop that sells old things for lots of money," says Carmen.

"Yes," says Luis. "But is it his shop? Or is he here to buy something? I guess there is only one way to find out."

"You mean go inside and talk to him? I don't know if that's safe," says Carmen. "The guy could do anything. He could attack us in there. No one would ever know. Maybe it's time to let the cops take over."

"What do we tell the cops?" says Luis. "Your card is gone. But we can't show them that this guy did it."

"That's not our job," says Carmen. "The cops can make him come clean."

"Well, if you say so. OK. You go call the cops," says Luis. "I will see to it that the guy doesn't leave."

Carmen makes the call. A cop car gets to the shop at 3:00. There are two cops in it. One of them gets out. Carmen tells him her story. He says, "You kids come in with me. Let's talk to the man. We will go from there."

The man comes out of the back when he hears the door ring. "Yes?" he says. "Can I help you?" Then he sees Carmen. "We meet again! I'm so happy!"

"You are?" says the cop.

"This is the man," says Carmen. "Take him in."

"Not so fast," says the cop. He asks the man, "Why are you so happy to see this girl?"

"Because she has something I want," says the

man. "We were at a sale together. There was an old wooden box I wanted, but she got to it first. I asked her to sell it to me. She would not even talk to me about it." He turns to Carmen. "Did you change your mind? Do you have the box with you now?"

"Forget about the box. What about the baseball card?" Carmen gives him a close look. But he just looks as if he doesn't know what she is talking about.

"What card?" he says. "I only want the box."

"Yes," says Carmen. "How much did you think you were going to buy it for?"

"What did I say before? $25? Maybe I can go up as far as $32."

"You would like that!" says Carmen. "What if I tell you the box has come apart? Now do you want it?"

"No problem. See all these?" He points to the back wall. Carmen sees box after box. They all look a little like the one she has. "This is what I do. I go around to sales. I buy old things made of wood. I make them look like new. Then I sell them for a little more. People like boxes like the one you have. That's what I was trying to tell you."

The cop has had all he can take. "No more about boxes," he cries out. "Did you or did you not take a baseball card from this girl?"

"No. I told you. No," says the man. "I don't know anything about a card. I just want the box. I can get as much as $200 for it, if I sell it here."

"But you wanted to give me $25 for it!" Carmen cries.

"Why not?" says the man. "I can't sell the box as is. I have to put a lot of work into it. My work is what makes these old boxes worth so much. Maybe I can give you as much as $40 for your box—but no more. Take it, or leave it. Now it's your turn. Why are you here with a cop? What's this about a card?"

"Wait," says Luis. "I saw you outside Carmen's house. I saw you write something down. What was that all about?"

"I just wanted to write her a letter," says the man. "I wanted to tell her all the things I have just told you. I did write that letter. Here." He gives a letter to the cop.

The cop reads the letter. "Well," he says, "this is just what the man says it is."

"Anyway," the man goes on, "why would I want a card? I don't sell cards."

The cop looks around. "Right again. I see a lot of boxes, but no cards. Your story I believe." He turns to Carmen. "Your story, on the other hand, doesn't sound on the up and up. Carmen? Is that your name? I'm going to tell you something, Carmen. Don't you ever play games with cops again. We don't like it. I'll let it go this time, but there had better not be a next time."

The cop takes his leave.

"Let's go," says Luis.

But Carmen says, "Wait." She says to the man, "All right. I'll sell you the box for $40. What if I throw in the other card?"

"What other card?" says Luis.

"Didn't I tell you? Another part of the box came off. There was another baseball card in that part. Another old one. From 1901, I think. She turns back to the man. "I'll sell you the box for $40—without the card. But if you want the card, I will ask $10 more. What do you think of that? The box and the card for $50?"

The man laughs. "$10 for a baseball card? I

don't think so! Just sell me the box, and I'll be happy."

"Really? You don't want the card? I could let you have it for $5," says Carmen.

The man laughs again. "You don't get it, do you? I don't sell baseball cards. I don't even like baseball. Ball One...Ball Two...nothing ever happens in that game. For all I know, the card is worth nothing. If you want to sell me the box, good. If not, let's part as friends."

Luis says, "You're wrong about baseball. You should see me play."

"I have better things to do."

Carmen says, "Come on, Luis. Let's go."

Outside, Luis says, "Can you believe that guy? Did you hear what he said about baseball?"

"Yes," says Carmen. "I believe him in more ways than one—sad to say."

"About the card, you mean?"

"You got it. That man did not take my card. He really doesn't know what a baseball card can be worth."

"Is there another card, Carmen?"

"No, but he doesn't know that. Where there is one card, there may be two. If he took the first card, he would want this one, too."

"Where does this leave you?" Luis asks.

"Back where I started." She looks at Luis. "Will you drive me home?"

16. Bad Dog, Cougar!

Carmen walks into the house with Luis. She has asked him in for something to drink. After all, he did try to help her. She hears Inez screaming in another part of the house. She hears her grandma saying something, too. Then there is a big sound. The dog comes through the door, going fast. It has something in its mouth again.

Grandma comes through the door after the dog. "Your no good dog has our fish. That was going to be our dinner!"

"Oh, no!" Carmen starts to get up, but the dog races by.

"Forget it," says Grandma. "We can't have that fish now, anyway. Not after it has been in a dog's mouth."

Luis says, "That's the same dog that was

at Mom's. It took food away from some guy there."

"Yes," says Carmen. "Cougar is not a good dog, I'm sorry to say. He takes things all the time."

"Where does he take them?" Luis asks.

"I don't know. He has his own dog door. He runs out the back."

"Would he take my pack," Luis asks, "if I leave it over there?"

"If you don't want him to have it, yes, he will take it," says Carmen. "If you want something, he wants it, too. Come to think of it, he is like Inez and me. So don't leave your pack there."

"Does he know what you're saying?"

"Cougar is a dog, Luis!"

"I know. But he may know more than you think. Let's talk where he can't hear us." Carmen takes Luis to the kitchen. There Luis says, "I want to try something. You go outside. I'll wait for the dog to come out. See where he goes."

Carmen goes outside. Luis sits down. He puts his pack next to him. He looks at Cougar. "Bad dog!" he says. "Don't take this!" Then he looks away. The dog sits for a while, looking at Luis.

Then the dog comes closer. Luis does not move. The dog comes closer, closer. Then in one fast move, he races up. He gets the pack in his mouth. He races away. Luis runs after him, screaming, "Bad dog! Get back here!"

Outside, Carmen is waiting behind a wall. She sees Cougar come through his dog door. Cougar has to pull hard to get the pack through the door. Then he runs around the house. Carmen runs after him. She is just in time to see Cougar go behind an old smashed-up car. The car has been there as long as Carmen can remember.

Luis comes out. He says, "Where did he go?"

Carmen points. "But it can't be," she says.

"Try," says Luis. "Go. Just have a look."

Carmen goes around the old car. Then she stops.

There sits Cougar with the pack and the fish. When he sees Carmen, he takes the pack in his mouth and moves back. He thinks this is a game. He wants to play. But Carmen is not looking at Cougar. She is looking at the things next to the fish. There is the ring Grandma lost. There is her homework from the other day. **There** is her own $22,000 baseball card.

17. Carmen and Luis

One day, Luis comes to see Carmen. They sit around in her room. They talk about this and that. Luis smiles and laughs as always. But Carmen can tell that he is not happy. "What's wrong?" she asks.

"Oh, nothing," he says. "I would just like to be someone else, not me. Things just don't work out for me, ever. I wanted to be your boyfriend, but you're going out with Tom. I wanted to get on the baseball team. They will not have me. I have to face it, Carmen. I'm a big nothing. There is only one thing I can do really well: I can make people laugh."

"You're a big something to me," says Carmen. "Yes, you make people laugh. But is that so bad? That's what you **try** to do. Isn't it, Luis? Be happy that it works. Everyone likes you for it. I do."

"You do?" he looks up.

"Yes—I—I **really** like you, Luis. After all, everyone gets sad at times. When I'm sad, I need a laugh more than anything."

Luis smiles. "So, I'm always good for a laugh?"

"I didn't mean it that way," says Carmen. "You do lots of things well. You paint, don't you? You're a good guy, Luis. Give it time. All the things you want will happen."

"Will they?" says Luis. "I want to be the best player on the team—any team. Is that going to happen? I want people to look up to me. I want them to get out of my way when they see me coming. I want them to say: Here comes Luis. That guy can really walk the walk. I want to be like your boyfriend, Tom. Will that ever happen? Who am I kidding?"

"Tom has his thing," says Carmen. "You have your thing. People are not all the same. Anyway, you're not the only who ever feels this way. How about me? What am I good at?"

"You?" says Luis. "You're good at being good to people. You're not always thinking of yourself. That makes you one in 1,000,000. If I ever have a problem, you're the one I want next to me because you don't back down. You don't get scared. Nothing gets to you."

"Well, what do you know!" says Carmen. "I would say all the same things about you, Luis. By the way, Tom is not my boyfriend anymore."

"What?" Luis just looks at her, his mouth open. "How did that happen?"

"How does it ever happen? He got mad at me. I got mad at him. End of story."

Luis does not know what to say. As he is looking for the words, Inez comes in. "Carmen. It's Tom calling."

"What does he want?" Carmen asks.

"He says he will forget all the bad things you have said and done," Inez tells her. "He says he will be your boyfriend again. But you have to do two things. You have to tell him you're sorry. You have to give him $650."

"Is that all?" says Carmen. "Did he just hear about the card or something?"

"Yes," says Inez. "He knows you have money in the bank. Do you want to talk to him? He is on the line."

"No," says Carmen. "Tell Tom I will get back to him."

But Inez does not leave. She keeps looking at Carmen and Luis. "Say," she asks at last, "just what is going on here? With you and Luis, I mean?"

"Nothing." says Carmen. "Go now."

But Inez can see that something is going on. She can tell from the way Carmen is looking at Luis. So now Inez looks at Luis, too. She asks herself why she did not see this before. Luis is Carmen's friend. He does not want money the way Tom does. He wants what is best for Carmen! For the first time, it hits Inez. It isn't Tom she really wants. It's Luis!

"Carmen—" she says.

"No," says Carmen. "The answer is no. Why do you even ask?"